Love's Broken Compass: Reclaiming Your Direction After a Heartbreak

Pasindu A

Published by Creative2Hemispheres, 2024.

LOVE'S BROKEN COMPASS: RECLAIMING YOUR DIRECTION AFTER A HEARTBREAK

First edition. March 10, 2024.

ISBN: 979-8224926992

Written by Pasindu A.

Also by Pasindu A

Find the Man of Your Dreams: 10 Traits of High-Value Men

Miles Apart Hearts Together: 10 Ways to Thrive in a Long Distance Relationship

Financial Planning for the Modern Couple: 10 Ways to Manage Your Finances in Today's Economy

The Disaster Preparedness Survival Guide: 10 Tips on How to Plan and Prepare for Any Emergency

The Secret to a Great Sex Life

The Science of Attraction

Love's Broken Compass: Reclaiming Your Direction After a Heartbreak

Watch for more at https://healthfactsbydoctorpasindu.com/.

Table of Contents

To all my readers who encourage me to write!

Love's Broken Compass

Reclaiming Your Direction After a Heartbreak

PASINDU A

Foreword: Unfurling the Map After Love's Storm

ove, in its purest form, is a beautiful and powerful force. However, the path of love is not always smooth sailing. When a relationship falters and a heartbreak sets in, it can feel like your emotional compass has been shattered, leaving you lost and disoriented in a sea of uncertainty. You might find yourself questioning everything you thought you knew about love, relationships, and even yourself.

Love's Broken Compass is not just another "get over it" guide. This book is your lifeline in the storm, offering more than just words of comfort. It's a comprehensive guide packed with **10 powerful tools** to help you navigate the challenging terrain of heartbreak and emerge stronger on the other side.

Here's what you can expect:

- **Validation, not platitudes:** This book acknowledges the depth of your pain and the unique challenges you face.
- **Practical strategies, not empty promises:** Each chapter equips you with actionable steps and proven techniques to navigate the emotional rollercoaster of heartbreak.
- **Hope, not despair:** This book guides you towards a future filled with hope and the possibility of finding love again.

Whether you're in the throes of fresh heartbreak or still healing from past wounds, **Love's Broken Compass** will be your trusted companion. As you turn the pages, you'll discover:

- How to navigate the emotional storms of heartbreak with **grace**

and resilience

- How to **reconnect with your inner strength** and rediscover your authentic self
- How to **transform your pain into a catalyst** for personal growth and positive change
- How to cultivate **gratitude and optimism** to pave the way for a brighter future

This book is not a magic bullet, but it's a powerful compass to guide you back to your true north. With **compassionate guidance, insightful exercises, and real-life stories,** Love's Broken Compass empowers you to reclaim your direction, rebuild your heart, and open yourself to the possibility of love once again.

Are you ready to begin your journey of healing and rediscover the strength and resilience that lies within you?

Then embark on this voyage with Love's Broken Compass and start charting a new course towards a future filled with love, happiness, and self-discovery.

Introduction

The sting of heartbreak. It's a phrase we've all heard, a sensation we've all, at some point, felt. It can be a sharp, searing pain that steals the breath from your lungs, or a dull ache that lingers in the background, a constant reminder of what you've lost.

Love, in all its glorious complexity, can also be the source of immense pain. When a relationship ends, especially one that holds deep meaning and hope, the world can shift on its axis, leaving us feeling lost and unsure of where to go next.

This experience, however universal, is deeply personal. It's a journey we each navigate in our unique way, grappling with the emotional turmoil and searching for a path forward.

This book is not a magic wand to erase the pain of heartbreak. It is, however, a compass, a guide to help you navigate the storm, find solid ground, and ultimately, reclaim your direction. As a doctor and a relationship coach, I have witnessed firsthand the resilience of the human spirit, and through these pages, I offer you the tools and strategies I've seen work for countless individuals facing heartbreak.

Together, we'll explore the emotional and psychological terrain of heartbreak, learn to navigate the grieving process, and ultimately, chart a new course toward a future filled with self-compassion, resilience, and the potential for new beginnings.

So, take a deep breath, turn the page, and let's embark on this journey together.

Chapter 1: Charting the Storm - Understanding the Impact of Heartbreak

Heartbreak. A single word that carries a universe of emotions - a gut-wrenching cocktail of sadness, anger, despair, and confusion. It's a universal experience, a storm we all weather at some point in our lives. But while universal, heartbreak is also deeply personal. Its impact on our emotional, psychological, and physical well-being is unique to each of us.

This chapter is your roadmap as you navigate the initial turbulence of heartbreak. We'll explore the emotional rollercoaster you're likely experiencing, understand the psychological changes that can occur, and even delve into the surprising physical effects of a broken heart.

Most importantly, we'll validate your emotions. Heartbreak is a legitimate form of grief, and the pain you feel is real. Ignoring or suppressing these feelings will only prolong the healing process.

Here, you'll gain a deeper understanding of the grieving journey, allowing you to navigate it with self-compassion and awareness.

The Emotional Rollercoaster

The emotional response to heartbreak is often described as a rollercoaster. One moment you might be consumed by sadness, the next, a wave of anger washes over you. Here's a closer look at some of the key emotions you might be experiencing:

- **Sadness:** This is the most common emotion associated with heartbreak. You might feel a deep sense of loss, longing for the past, or a pervasive emptiness. Tears are a natural response, a way for your body to release emotional pain.

- **Anger:** It's normal to feel angry at your former partner, especially if the relationship ended abruptly or due to betrayal. This anger can also be directed inward, leading to self-blame or feelings of inadequacy.
- **Denial:** Sometimes, the reality of the situation is too overwhelming to accept. Denial may manifest as pretending everything is okay, minimizing the seriousness of the breakup, or clinging to the hope of reconciliation.
- **Guilt:** You might blame yourself for things that went wrong in the relationship, leading to overwhelming guilt. It's important to learn from past experiences, but don't shoulder all the blame.
- **Loneliness:** Feeling isolated and alone is a common experience during heartbreak. You might miss the companionship and intimacy of your former partner, or feel disconnected from friends and family due to emotional withdrawal.
- **Jealousy:** If your ex-partner moves on quickly, you might experience jealousy. This can be particularly painful if they seem to be happy without you.
- **Confusion:** Trying to make sense of what happened and why the relationship ended can leave you feeling confused and disoriented.

These emotions are all valid and deserve acknowledgement. Remember, there's no right or wrong way to feel.

The Psychological Shift

Heartbreak doesn't just affect our emotions; it can also have a significant impact on our psychological well-being. Here are some common experiences:

- **Loss of Identity:** During a relationship, our sense of self can become intertwined with our partner's. Heartbreak can force us to re-evaluate who we are as individuals, which can be a daunting but ultimately growth-promoting experience.
- **Difficulty Concentrating:** The emotional turmoil of heartbreak can make it hard to focus on work, studies, or daily tasks.
- **Decreased Motivation:** Feeling lost and demotivated is common. Activities that used to bring you joy may lose their appeal.
- **Disrupted Sleep Patterns:** Sleep disturbances like insomnia or excessive sleep are common after a breakup.
- **Changes in Appetite:** Some people lose their appetite, while others experience emotional eating. These unhealthy coping mechanisms are best dealt with through self-care practices.

The Physical Toll

Believe it or not, heartbreak can manifest in physical ways as well. Your body experiences a stress response similar to that of a physical injury. Here are some common physical effects:

- **Fatigue:** The emotional and psychological drain of heartbreak can leave you feeling constantly exhausted.
- **Headaches and body aches:** The stress response can lead to muscle tension and headaches.
- **Weakened Immune System:** Heartbreak can temporarily weaken your immune system, making you more susceptible to illness.
- **Changes in Appetite and Digestion:** As mentioned earlier, changes in appetite and digestive problems are common during emotional distress.

- **Chest Pain and Shortness of Breath:** The stress hormone cortisol can trigger chest tightness or a feeling of shortness of breath. While these can be scary, they are usually harmless.

If you experience any concerning physical symptoms, it's important to consult your doctor to rule out any underlying medical conditions.

Understanding the Grieving Process

Heartbreak is a form of grief. You're grieving the loss of the relationship, the future you envisioned together and the dreams and hopes you shared. Grief is a natural and necessary process for healing. Just as with any loss, the grieving process following heartbreak unfolds in stages, but it's important to remember that these stages are not linear and everyone experiences them differently.

Here's a general framework of the grieving process, keeping in mind that it's not a rigid structure:

1. Denial: This initial stage is a way for your mind and body to cope with the shock of the breakup. You might deny the reality of the situation, holding onto the hope of reconciliation.

2. Anger: As the initial shock subsides, anger often emerges. You might be angry at your ex-partner, yourself, or even the situation itself.

3. Bargaining: This stage involves a desperate attempt to regain control and undo the loss. You might find yourself bargaining with yourself, your ex-partner, or a higher power, making promises or offering sacrifices in exchange for a chance to get back together.

4. Depression: This is often the most intense stage, characterized by feelings of sadness, despair, and hopelessness. You might lose interest in activities you once enjoyed, withdraw from social interaction, and experience changes in appetite and sleep.

5. Acceptance: This final stage doesn't necessarily mean you're happy about the breakup or have completely moved on. Instead, it signifies an acceptance of reality and a willingness to move forward with your life.

While this is a general framework, remember that your journey will be unique. You may not experience all five stages, and the order can vary. There might be periods of regression, where you revisit earlier stages. This is all entirely normal.

The most important takeaway is to be kind to yourself throughout this process. Acknowledge your emotions, don't judge yourself for feeling them, and trust that you will eventually heal.

Validating Your Emotions

Throughout this chapter, we've explored the emotional, psychological, and physical effects of heartbreak. It's important to reiterate that the pain you're experiencing is real and valid. Don't let anyone tell you otherwise, and don't try to minimize your feelings.

Suppressing emotions only prolongs the healing process. Instead, allow yourself to feel your emotions fully. Cry if you need to, express your anger in a healthy way, and reach out for support from trusted friends and family.

Healing from heartbreak takes time, and there will be good days and bad days. This chapter is just the beginning of your journey. In the following chapters, we'll delve deeper into strategies to navigate the emotional turmoil, practice self-care, and ultimately, reclaim your direction and rebuild your life.

Remember, you are not alone in this. With self-compassion, resilience, and the tools offered in the coming chapters, you will emerge from this storm stronger and ready to embrace new beginnings.

Chapter 2: Finding Solid Ground - Accepting and Letting Go

The aftermath of a breakup can feel like an emotional earthquake, leaving you shaken and unsure of where to stand. In Chapter 2, we'll focus on finding solid ground - accepting the reality of the relationship's end and letting go of the idea of what could have been. This doesn't mean burying your emotions or pretending the relationship didn't matter. It's about acknowledging the pain, processing your feelings in a healthy way, and ultimately moving forward with acceptance and resilience.

Accepting Reality: The First Step Towards Healing

Acceptance is not about condoning your ex-partner's actions or minimizing your own hurt. It's about acknowledging the truth of the situation - the relationship has ended. Denial, on the other hand, keeps you stuck in a cycle of emotional turmoil. By clinging to the past and holding onto false hope, you delay the healing process.

Here's why accepting reality is crucial:

- **Empowers You:** Acceptance puts you back in control of your emotions and your future.
- **Reduces Emotional Distress:** Denial fuels anger, sadness, and anxiety. Accepting reality allows you to begin processing your emotions in a healthy way.
- **Paves the Way for Healing:** Acceptance is the foundation for moving on and creating a fulfilling future.

Letting Go of the "What Ifs"

A significant part of acceptance involves letting go of the "what ifs" - the fantasies of what your relationship could have been if things had been different. Dwelling on these hypothetical scenarios keeps you emotionally attached to the past and hinders your ability to move forward. Here's how to let go of the "what ifs":

- **Recognize the Futility:** Recognize that dwelling on the past won't change anything. The relationship is over, and focusing on what could have been is an exercise in futility.
- **Shift Your Focus:** Instead of ruminating on the past, focus on the present and the future. What are your goals and aspirations? What steps can you take to create a fulfilling life for yourself?
- **Practice Forgiveness:** Forgiveness doesn't condone your ex-partner's actions or erase the hurt you experienced. It's about releasing the anger and resentment that can hold you back from moving forward.

Building Healthy Coping Mechanisms

Journaling:

Journaling is a powerful tool for processing emotions and making sense of your experiences. Regularly writing about your thoughts and feelings can help you:

- **Gain Clarity:** Journaling allows you to explore the depths of your emotions and identify recurring themes or patterns.
- **Release Emotions:** The act of writing itself can be a cathartic experience, allowing you to release pent-up emotions in a safe space.
- **Track Progress:** Over time, reviewing your journal entries can reveal progress in your healing journey.

Example: After a painful breakup, Sarah started journaling every night. She wrote about her feelings of sadness, anger, and confusion. Through journaling, Sarah realized that she felt a sense of resentment towards her ex for not prioritizing the relationship. By identifying this emotion, Sarah was able to begin processing it and eventually let go of the anger.

Mindfulness Practices:

Mindfulness practices like meditation and deep breathing can help manage difficult emotions and cultivate emotional regulation. In heartbreak's throes, your mind might be racing with negative thoughts. Mindfulness helps you become more present in the moment, observe your thoughts and feelings without judgment, and gradually detach from emotional overwhelm.

Exercise: Mindfulness practices can be as simple as focusing on your breath during a short meditation session. Deep breathing exercises can be particularly helpful when you're feeling overwhelmed with emotions.

Example: David, struggling with anxiety after his breakup, decided to try meditation. He downloaded a guided meditation app and started practicing mindfulness exercises for 10 minutes each day. As he focused on his breath and observed his thoughts without judgment, David noticed a gradual decrease in his anxiety and a sense of calm washing over him.

Seeking Support:

Don't underestimate the power of human connection. Surrounding yourself with supportive friends, family, or a therapist can provide a safe space to express your emotions and feel less alone.

- **Friends and Family:** Talk to loved ones who can offer a listening ear and words of encouragement.
- **Support Groups:** Joining a support group for people going

through breakups can connect you with others who understand your pain and offer valuable advice.

- **Therapy:** Seeking professional help from a therapist can be especially beneficial if you're struggling to cope with the emotional aftermath of the breakup.

Example: Olivia, feeling isolated after her breakup, decided to reconnect with her close friends. They organized movie nights, went for walks together, and simply offered Olivia their presence and support. Talking to her friends allowed Olivia to express her emotions openly and feel a sense of belonging during this challenging time. Additionally, Olivia began attending a support group for individuals going through breakups. Sharing her experiences with others who understood her pain helped Olivia feel less alone and gain valuable insights into navigating this difficult phase in her life.

Remember:

- **Healing is not linear:** There will be good days and bad days. Be patient with yourself and allow yourself to feel your emotions.
- **Set boundaries:** It's okay to limit contact with your ex-partner if necessary, especially if it hinders your healing process.
- **Practice self-care:** Prioritize activities that nourish your physical and mental well-being, such as healthy eating, regular exercise, and getting enough sleep.
- **Celebrate small victories:** Acknowledge your progress, no matter how small. Each step you take towards healing is a victory.

By accepting the reality of the situation, letting go of the "what ifs," and building healthy coping mechanisms, you'll gradually begin to navigate the path towards healing and emerge stronger and more resilient.

Remember, you are not alone. Lean on your support system, embrace self-compassion, and trust that with time and effort, you will find your way back to a place of peace and happiness.

In the next chapter, we'll delve into recalibrating your compass - redefining your values and priorities to create a new vision for your future independent of the relationship. This chapter will guide you in rediscovering what truly matters to you and charting a course towards a fulfilling life.

Chapter 3: Recalibrating the Compass - Redefining Your Values and Priorities

The storm of heartbreak can leave you feeling disoriented and unsure of where you're headed. In Chapter 3, we'll focus on recalibrating your compass, rediscovering your core values and aspirations, and creating a new vision for yourself independent of the relationship.

A relationship can have a profound impact on our sense of self. Sometimes, we become so intertwined with our partner that our own goals and values get blurred.

Now, as you navigate the journey of healing, it's crucial to rediscover who you are at your core and what truly matters to you.

This chapter will equip you with the tools to:

- **Engage in self-reflection.**
- **Identify your core values.**
- **Define your personal vision for the future.**

Embracing Self-Reflection

Self-reflection is the foundation of personal growth. It's about taking a deep dive into your inner world, understanding your motivations, and identifying what brings you meaning and fulfillment. Here are some strategies to embark on this journey:

- **Journaling:** Regular journaling can be a powerful tool for self-discovery. Spend time writing about your emotions, experiences, and aspirations. Explore recurring themes, patterns, and situations that evoke strong feelings. This allows you to observe patterns and gain clarity on your thoughts and feelings.

- **Mindfulness practices:** Practices like meditation can help you quiet your mind and connect with your inner self. By becoming more present in the moment, focusing on your breath and bodily sensations, you can gain a clearer understanding of your values and desires.

- **Strengths assessments:** Online or self-guided strengths assessments can reveal your natural talents and abilities. Knowing your strengths can help you identify areas you want to develop and paths you might want to pursue. Explore resources like the VIA Character Strengths Survey, which identifies 24 character strengths that can be valuable assets in various aspects of life.

- **Seek external perspectives:** Talking to trusted friends, mentors, or a therapist can provide valuable insights into your personality and goals. Sharing your experiences and thought processes with supportive individuals can offer new perspectives and help you identify patterns you might have missed.

Example: After a breakup that left her feeling lost, Maya started journaling every morning. She wrote about her feelings of sadness and confusion, but also explored memories of times she felt happy, fulfilled, and proud of herself.

Through this process, Maya realized that a career in environmental conservation, a passion she had neglected while in her relationship, truly resonated with her. Additionally, she sought guidance from a career counselor who identified Maya's strengths in analytical thinking, problem-solving, and leadership. Together, they explored potential career paths within the environmental field that aligned with Maya's values and skillset.

Unearthing Your Core Values

Your core values are the fundamental principles that guide your decisions and actions. They represent what's most important to you and what defines your sense of integrity. Here's how to identify your core values:

- **Reflect on past experiences:** Consider times when you felt happy, fulfilled, or proud of yourself. What values were present in those situations? For instance, if you felt happy volunteering at an animal shelter, perhaps compassion and animal welfare are core values for you.

- **Imagine your ideal life:** Envision your perfect life five or ten years from now. What elements are essential to this ideal future? What values would be necessary to achieve this vision? Perhaps you see yourself living in a bustling city, pursuing a creative career. This might indicate that values like independence, creativity, and intellectual stimulation are important to you.

- **Consider role models:** Who do you admire? What values do they embody that resonate with you? Examining the qualities you admire in others, can provide clues about your own values. Perhaps you admire a historical figure known for their courage or a friend known for their unwavering loyalty. These qualities might represent values you hold dear.

- **Use a values list:** Explore online resources or self-help books that provide lists of core values. Some common core values include honesty, compassion, adventure, creativity, integrity, and family. Mark the values that resonate most with you and consider why they are important to you.

Example: During his self-reflection process, Alex realized that some of his core values included adventure, intellectual growth, and personal freedom. He noticed that these values often took a backseat while in his relationship, leading to a sense of personal stagnation. By identifying his core values, Alex gained clarity on what truly mattered to him and what he wanted to prioritize in his future. He envisioned himself traveling the world, learning new languages, and potentially pursuing a career in international relations, a field that would allow him to explore different cultures and engage in intellectual pursuits.

Building Your Vision for the Future

Now that you've embarked on self-reflection and identified your core values, it's time to create a vision board for your future - a personalized roadmap representing your hopes and aspirations. Here's how:

- **Brainstorm:** Spend some time brainstorming possibilities. What do you want your life to look like in different aspects - career, relationships, personal growth, hobbies, etc.? Don't be afraid to dream big at this stage. Envision yourself achieving your goals and living a life that aligns with your values.
- **Gather inspiration:** Collect images, quotes, or anything that visually represents your aspirations. Explore magazines, websites, or even nature for inspiration. Look for visuals that evoke feelings of excitement, motivation, and fulfillment. You can also include personal items that hold sentimental value and remind you of your goals.
- **Create a visual board:** Physically or digitally organize your collected images and words into a visual representation of your ideal future. If creating a physical board, use a poster board, corkboard, or any other flat surface. Arrange your visuals in a way that is aesthetically pleasing and inspires you. If opting for a

digital board, use online tools like Pinterest or Canva to create a collage.

- **Review regularly:** Revisit your vision board regularly to keep your goals at the forefront of your mind and stay motivated. Remember, your vision can evolve over time, so feel free to update it as your priorities shift and your dreams take shape. Regularly reviewing your vision board can serve as a reminder of your aspirations and encourage you to take action towards making them a reality.

Example: Sarah, after identifying her core values of creativity, financial stability, and independence, created a vision board. It included images of a flourishing art studio, travel destinations she'd always dreamed of visiting, and financial planning resources.

Additionally, she included a quote: "Perhaps travel cannot prevent bigotry, but by demonstrating that all people cry, laugh, eat, worry, and die, it can introduce the idea that if we try and understand each other, we may even become friends."

This quote resonated with Sarah's value of personal growth and her desire to experience new cultures and perspectives. By regularly reviewing her vision board, Sarah stayed motivated to pursue an art career, make sound financial decisions, and plan future adventures that would allow her to broaden her horizons and connect with diverse individuals.

Remember:

- Redefining your values and creating a vision board are ongoing processes. Be patient with yourself, and allow your goals and aspirations to evolve as you grow and learn.
- Celebrate your progress, no matter how small. Each step you take towards your vision is a step in the right direction.

Recognizing and acknowledging your progress can boost your motivation and keep you moving forward on your journey of self-discovery and personal growth.

This chapter has equipped you with tools for self-reflection, value identification, and vision building. By delving into your inner world, you've begun the process of reclaiming your sense of self and charting a new course for your future.

Remember, you are the author of your own story. Embrace your individuality, prioritize what truly matters to you, and move forward with unwavering hope and a renewed sense of purpose.

In the next chapter, we'll delve into practical strategies for rebuilding your life after heartbreak. We'll explore that Self-care is not only indulging in fleeting pleasures but also about nurturing your physical, emotional, and mental well-being to create a solid foundation for growth and healing.

Chapter 4: Repairing the Sails - Self-Care and Emotional Healing

Navigating the emotional storm of heartbreak requires resilience and self-compassion. In Chapter 4, we'll focus on "repairing the sails" - building resilience through self-care practices and prioritizing emotional healing.

Self-care is not about indulging in fleeting pleasures. It's about nurturing your physical, emotional, and mental well-being to create a solid foundation for growth and healing. This chapter will explore various self-care practices to help you:

- Prioritize your physical health.
- Engage in activities that bring you joy and fulfillment.
- Seek professional help when needed.

Nurturing Your Body

Your body is the vessel for your emotions and experiences. Taking care of your physical health is crucial for emotional well-being and overall resilience. Here are some key areas to focus on:

- **Healthy Eating:** Nourish your body with nutritious foods that provide energy and support your immune system. This doesn't mean following an overly restrictive diet, but rather making conscious choices that promote overall health. Include a variety of fruits, vegetables, whole grains, and lean protein in your diet. Limit processed foods, sugary drinks, and unhealthy fats.
- **Regular Exercise:** Physical activity is a powerful mood booster and stress reliever. It releases endorphins, natural mood-

elevating chemicals in the brain, and helps manage stress hormones. Find an exercise regimen you genuinely enjoy, whether it's dancing to your favorite music, taking a brisk walk in the nature, joining a fitness class, or practicing yoga. Even small amounts of daily activity, like taking the stairs or going for a short walk during your lunch break, can make a positive difference.

- **Quality Sleep:** Aim for 7-8 hours of quality sleep each night. Establishing a regular sleep schedule and creating a relaxing bedtime routine can improve your sleep quality. This routine might include taking a warm bath, reading a book, or practicing relaxation techniques like deep breathing or meditation before bed. Ensure your bedroom is dark, quiet, and cool to promote optimal sleep conditions.

Example: After a painful breakup, Olivia felt lethargic and had difficulty concentrating at work. She decided to prioritize her physical health, starting by meal prepping healthy lunches with a variety of colorful vegetables, lean protein like grilled chicken, and whole grains like brown rice. Olivia also joined a Zumba class with her friends, discovering that dancing not only helped her get exercise but also provided a fun and social outlet for stress relief. Additionally, she established a relaxing bedtime routine, including taking a warm bath and reading a book before bed, which significantly improved her sleep quality and overall energy levels.

Engaging in Activities You Enjoy

Engaging in activities you find enjoyable is crucial for boosting mood, reducing stress, and fostering a sense of fulfillment. Here are some ideas:

- **Hobbies:** Rediscover old hobbies you used to enjoy or explore new ones that spark your interest. Whether it's painting, playing music, reading, learning a new language, gardening, or volunteering for a cause you care about, engaging in activities you find fun and fulfilling can bring joy, a sense of accomplishment, and a healthy distraction from painful emotions.

- **Spending Time in Nature:** Immerse yourself in the beauty and tranquility of nature. Go for a walk in the park, hike in the woods, sit by a river, or simply spend time in your backyard observing your surroundings. Studies show that spending time in nature can significantly reduce stress, improve mood, and boost feelings of well-being. Breathe in the fresh air, listen to the sounds of nature, and allow yourself to disconnect from the constant stimulation of technology and daily pressures.

- **Socializing:** Surround yourself with supportive friends and family members who uplift and inspire you. Connect with loved ones who make you feel good about yourself, engage in shared activities, and offer emotional support during challenging times. Social connection can combat feelings of loneliness and isolation, fostering a sense of belonging and providing a safe space to share your emotions.

Example: David, after a difficult breakup, felt a sense of emptiness and a lack of direction. He decided to reconnect with his passion for playing the guitar, which he had neglected during his relationship. He also joined a local hiking group, finding solace in spending time in nature and connecting with like-minded individuals. Additionally, David made an effort to stay connected with his close friends, hosting game nights and attending social gatherings, which provided him with a sense of belonging and support during this challenging time.

Seeking Professional Help

Sometimes, the emotional challenges of heartbreak can feel overwhelming. If you're struggling to cope with the emotional turmoil, seeking professional help from a therapist or counselor is a sign of strength, not weakness. A therapist can provide a safe and confidential space to:

- Explore your emotions and understand their underlying causes.
- Develop healthy coping mechanisms for managing difficult emotions like sadness, anger, and anxiety.

- Identify and challenge negative thought patterns that might be hindering your healing process.
- Develop communication and relationship skills for building healthier relationships in the future.
- Learn mindfulness and relaxation techniques for stress management.

Here are some signs that professional help might be beneficial:

- **Feeling overwhelmed by sadness, anger, or anxiety that persists for weeks or months.**
- **Experiencing difficulty functioning in daily life, such as work, school, or social activities.**
- **Isolating yourself from social interactions and withdrawing from loved ones.**
- **Engaging in unhealthy coping mechanisms like substance abuse, self-harm, or risky behaviors.**
- **Having difficulty letting go of the past and moving forward.**

Remember, seeking professional help is an investment in your well-being. Don't hesitate to reach out and seek support if you need it. Therapists are trained professionals who can provide valuable guidance and support on your journey towards healing and emotional well-being.

Example: After months of struggling to move on from a difficult breakup, Emily felt overwhelmed by sadness, anxiety, and difficulty sleeping. She reached out to a therapist who specialized in relationship issues. Through therapy, Emily learned healthy coping mechanisms for managing her emotions, explored communication patterns in past relationships, and developed a clearer understanding of her needs and goals for future relationships. Therapy provided a safe space for Emily to process her emotions, gain insights into her experiences, and develop tools to build resilience and navigate future relationships with greater self-awareness and emotional maturity.

Conclusion

Prioritizing self-care is an ongoing journey, not a one-time fix. Experiment with different strategies, find what works best for you, and be patient with yourself. Remember, even small steps towards a healthier lifestyle and emotional well-being can have a significant impact on your healing process. As you nurture your body, engage in activities that bring you joy, and prioritize your emotional well-being, you'll gradually rebuild your resilience and emerge from this experience stronger and more equipped to navigate the journey of life with greater self-compassion and inner strength.

In the next chapter, we'll delve into building resilience and emotional intelligence, exploring strategies to manage difficult emotions and foster healthier relationships going forward.

Chapter 5: Mending the Rudder - Building Resilience and Emotional Intelligence

The emotional turbulence of heartbreak can leave you feeling adrift, unsure of how to navigate the challenges and complexities of life. In Chapter 5, we'll focus on "mending the rudder" - building resilience and emotional intelligence. These two crucial aspects equip you with the tools to weather future storms, foster healthier relationships, and cultivate a sense of well-being that transcends any relationship's ending.

Building Resilience: The Ability to Bounce Back

Resilience is the ability to adapt and thrive in the face of adversity. It's not about avoiding difficult emotions or challenges, but rather about developing the capacity to bounce back from them with strength and a sense of growth. Here are some key strategies to build resilience:

- **Cultivate a Growth Mindset:** Embrace the belief that your abilities and qualities are not fixed but can be developed through effort and learning. This growth mindset fosters resilience by encouraging you to see challenges as opportunities for learning and personal growth.

Example: After a painful breakup, Sarah initially felt defined by the failure of the relationship. However, she adopted a growth mindset, recognizing that the experience could teach her valuable lessons about communication, self-awareness, and emotional regulation. This shift in perspective empowered Sarah to view challenges as opportunities for self-improvement and growth.

- **Develop Healthy Coping Mechanisms:** While avoiding

difficult emotions might seem tempting, it's ultimately counterproductive. Instead, focus on developing healthy coping mechanisms that allow you to process emotions effectively and navigate challenging situations constructively. Some examples include:

- ○ **Physical Activity:** Exercise releases endorphins, natural mood-lifters that can improve your emotional well-being and reduce stress. Engaging in activities you enjoy, like dancing, swimming, or team sports, can also provide a sense of social connection and accomplishment.

- ○ **Mindfulness Practices:** Techniques like meditation and deep breathing can help you become more aware of your thoughts and emotions without judgment. This allows you to observe your emotional state calmly and choose a mindful response rather than reacting impulsively.

- ○ **Creative Expression:** Channeling your emotions into creative outlets like journaling, art, or music can be a cathartic experience, allowing you to express your feelings in a healthy way and gain a deeper understanding of your inner world.

- **Build a Strong Support System:** Surrounding yourself with supportive friends, family members, or a therapist can provide a safe space to express your emotions, receive validation, and gain valuable perspectives. Having a strong support system can foster a sense of belonging and connection, reminding you that you're not alone in navigating difficult times.

Example: David, feeling overwhelmed with emotional turmoil after his breakup, reached out to a close friend. Talking openly about his emotions and receiving support from his friend helped David feel less isolated and more equipped to cope with his feelings in a healthy way.

- **Practice Gratitude:** Taking time to appreciate the positive aspects of your life, even during challenging times, can shift your perspective and boost your resilience. Cultivating an attitude of gratitude reminds you of the blessings you already possess and fosters a sense of optimism and hope for the future. Start a gratitude journal and jot down a few things you're grateful for each day, or share them verbally with loved ones.

Developing Emotional Intelligence: Understanding and Managing Emotions

Emotional intelligence (EQ) refers to your ability to understand and manage your own emotions, as well as the emotions of others. It encompasses various skills like self-awareness, self-regulation, social awareness, and relationship management. By developing your EQ, you become adept at navigating the complexities of human interaction, building healthy relationships, and maintaining emotional well-being.

Here's how to enhance your emotional intelligence:

- **Enhancing Self-Awareness:** The foundation of emotional intelligence is self-awareness, the ability to recognize your own emotions. Pay attention to your bodily sensations, thoughts, and behaviors throughout the day.

Example: Olivia began paying attention to her physical reactions when she felt overwhelmed. She noticed that her palms got sweaty, her heart rate increased, and her breathing became shallow. By recognizing these physical cues, Olivia could identify the onset of anxiety and take steps to manage it, such as practicing deep breathing exercises or engaging in a calming activity.

- **Challenging Negative Thought Patterns:** Our thoughts significantly influence our emotions and overall well-being. When faced with difficult situations, negative thought patterns can worsen your emotional state. Practice challenging these negative thoughts by questioning their validity and replacing them with more realistic and positive ones.

Example: After his breakup, David kept thinking, "I'm not good enough." Recognizing the negativity of this thought, he challenged it by focusing on his strengths and accomplishments. He reminded himself of positive feedback he received from past employers and friends, highlighting his capabilities and self-worth.

- **Developing Empathy:** Empathy is the ability to understand and share the feelings of others. By actively listening, observing nonverbal cues, and considering different perspectives, you can cultivate empathy and build stronger, more meaningful connections with others.

Example: Sarah, wanting to improve her communication with friends, practiced active listening. She focused on paying full attention to her friend's words, avoiding interrupting, and asking clarifying questions to ensure she understood their perspective. This approach strengthened Sarah's relationships by demonstrating genuine care and understanding.

- **Practicing Effective Communication:** Clear and honest communication is essential for building and maintaining healthy relationships. This involves expressing your thoughts and feelings assertively, while also actively listening to and respecting the viewpoints of others.

Example: David, struggling to communicate his needs assertively in past relationships, decided to learn more about communication techniques. He practiced expressing his feelings directly and respectfully, avoiding passive-aggressive behavior or blaming language. This newfound skill helped David navigate future relationships with greater clarity and avoid misunderstandings.

Remember:

- Building resilience and emotional intelligence is a continuous process. It takes time, effort, and self-compassion to develop these essential skills. Celebrate your progress, no matter how small, and acknowledge the challenges you have overcome.

- Seeking professional help is a sign of strength, not weakness. If you're struggling to cope with difficult emotions or navigate challenging situations on your own, consider reaching out to a therapist or counselor. They can provide valuable guidance, support, and resources to help you on your journey towards emotional well-being and personal growth.

By "mending the rudder" - fostering resilience and emotional intelligence - you equip yourself with the tools to navigate life's complexities with greater confidence and clarity. You'll learn to manage your emotions effectively, communicate openly and honestly with others, and build stronger, more fulfilling relationships. Remember, you are not alone on this journey. Embrace the challenges as opportunities for growth, and trust that with time and effort, you'll emerge from this experience stronger, more resilient, and equipped to navigate the future with newfound emotional well-being.

Chapter 6: Navigating Uncharted Waters - Forgiveness and Self-Compassion

The aftermath of a breakup can feel like venturing into uncharted waters, leaving you unsure of the direction to take and how to navigate the emotional currents. In Chapter 6, we'll delve into the importance of forgiveness, both for yourself and the other person, and how self-compassion can serve as a guiding light on your journey towards healing.

Letting Go of the Anchor: Embracing Self-Forgiveness

Holding onto resentment and self-blame can weigh you down like an anchor, hindering your ability to move forward. Self-forgiveness is not about condoning your actions or minimizing the hurt you experienced. It's about acknowledging your role in the situation, taking responsibility for your mistakes, and ultimately releasing the burden of self-criticism.

Here's why self-forgiveness is crucial for healing:

- **Promotes Emotional Well-being:** Holding onto negativity can lead to anxiety, depression, and other mental health challenges. Letting go of self-blame allows you to experience emotional peace and move towards a state of well-being.
- **Empowers You:** Self-forgiveness empowers you to take control of your present and future. By releasing yourself from the past, you regain the ability to make choices that align with your values and create a fulfilling life.
- **Opens the Door to Growth:** Self-reflection and acknowledging your mistakes can be valuable learning experiences. By understanding your role in the relationship's

end, you can identify areas for personal growth and avoid repeating similar patterns in the future.

The Path to Self-Forgiveness:

- **Acknowledge Your Emotions:** The first step towards self-forgiveness is acknowledging your emotions honestly. Allow yourself to feel the hurt, anger, or sadness without judgment.
- **Take Responsibility:** Recognize your role in the relationship's challenges and any mistakes you might have made. This doesn't mean taking full responsibility for everything, but taking ownership of your actions and expressing remorse for any hurt you caused.
- **Practice Self-Compassion:** Treat yourself with the same kindness and understanding you would offer a loved one going through a similar situation. Forgive yourself for your imperfections and remember that everyone makes mistakes.
- **Reframe Negative Self-Talk:** Challenge negative self-criticism by replacing it with self-compassionate thoughts. Instead of saying, "I'm a failure," remind yourself that you're worthy of love and happiness, and that you have the strength to move forward.
- **Focus on the Present and Future:** While reflecting on the past can be beneficial for learning and growth, dwell too heavily on "what ifs" and regrets. Shift your focus to the present and future, setting positive intentions for your personal growth and future relationships.

The Art of Letting Go: Forgiveness Towards Others

Forgiving the other person doesn't mean condoning their actions or minimizing the pain they caused. It's about releasing the negative emotions associated with the situation and choosing not to let them control your life. Forgiveness is a gift you give to yourself, allowing you to move forward with peace and emotional freedom.

Here's why forgiveness is important for healing:

- **Reduces Emotional Distress:** Holding onto anger and resentment is emotionally draining. Forgiveness allows you to let go of these negative emotions, reducing stress and promoting overall well-being.
- **Empowers You:** Forgiveness takes back the power from the other person and their actions. It allows you to choose how you want to react and move forward with your life.
- **Promotes Personal Growth:** Forgiveness can create space for positive emotions like compassion and understanding. This fosters personal growth and allows you to cultivate healthier relationships in the future.

The Path to Forgiveness:

- **Understand the Process:** Forgiveness is a journey, not a destination. It takes time and effort, and there will be setbacks along the way. Be patient with yourself and allow the process to unfold naturally.
- **Separate the Person from the Action:** Remember that forgiveness is not about condoning the action itself. It's about choosing to let go of the negative emotions associated with that action and choosing not to let it define the other person or yourself.
- **Focus on Letting Go:** The purpose of forgiveness is not to forgive for the other person's benefit, but for your own. Focus on releasing the negativity and choosing peace for yourself.
- **Practice Compassion:** Try to understand the other person's

perspective and motivations, even if you don't condone their actions. This doesn't mean justifying their behavior, but rather acknowledging their humanity and acknowledging that people make mistakes.

- **Set Boundaries:** While forgiveness is crucial for your own healing, it doesn't necessarily mean reconciling with the other person. You have the right to set boundaries and protect your well-being, even if you've chosen to forgive them.

Self-Compassion: The Guiding Light

Self-compassion is treating yourself with the same kindness, understanding, and acceptance you would offer a close friend going through a difficult time. It involves acknowledging your struggles, understanding your vulnerabilities, and offering yourself support and encouragement.

Here's how self-compassion benefits your healing journey:

- **Reduces Self-Criticism:** Self-compassion replaces negative self-talk with understanding and acceptance. This fosters a more positive self-image and promotes emotional well-being.
- **Boosts Resilience:** Self-compassion allows you to cope with challenges and setbacks in a healthy way. By being kind to yourself, you build resilience and the strength to navigate difficult situations.
- **Promotes Positive Relationships:** When you treat yourself with compassion, you're more likely to extend the same kindness to others, fostering healthier and more fulfilling relationships.

Practicing Self-Compassion:

- **Mindfulness Meditation:** Mindfulness practices like meditation can help you observe your thoughts and feelings with non-judgmental awareness. This allows you to acknowledge your emotions without getting caught up in negative self-criticism.
- **Loving-Kindness Meditation:** This meditation practice involves sending positive messages of kindness and compassion to yourself. By repeating affirmations like "May I be safe, may I be happy, may I be healthy," you can cultivate self-love and acceptance.
- **Self-Soothing Activities:** Engage in activities that bring you comfort and relaxation, such as spending time in nature, listening to calming music, or taking a long bath. Prioritizing self-care activities demonstrates your commitment to your well-being.

Remember:

- **Healing is not linear:** There will be good days and bad days. Be patient with yourself and allow yourself to feel your emotions.
- **Seek support:** Don't be afraid to reach out to a therapist or counselor for professional guidance on your journey towards forgiveness and self-compassion.
- **You are not alone:** Many individuals have grappled with the challenges of navigating a breakup. Remember that you have the inner strength and resources to heal and move forward with a sense of hope and optimism.

By embracing self-forgiveness and forgiveness towards the other person, while cultivating self-compassion along the way, you navigate the uncharted waters of post-breakup life with greater clarity and emotional well-being.

Remember, forgiveness is not about condoning the past but about empowering yourself to create a fulfilling future. Embrace the lessons learned, choose to move forward with kindness towards yourself and others, and trust that brighter days lie ahead.

Chapter 7: Setting Sail Again - Reconnecting with Your Support System

The aftermath of a breakup can leave you feeling adrift, lost in a sea of emotions. Reconnecting with your support system is an essential step in navigating the emotional currents and setting sail again towards a fulfilling life. This chapter explores the importance of social connection, highlighting the roles that friends, family, support groups, and even professional help can play in your healing journey.

The Power of Connection: Humans are Wired for Social Connection

Humans are social creatures, with inherent needs for belonging, validation, and emotional connection. Our brains are wired to thrive in social settings, and strong social bonds contribute significantly to emotional and mental well-being. During challenging times like a breakup, the support of loved ones becomes even more crucial. Here's why social connection matters when healing from a breakup:

- **Combating Loneliness and Isolation:** A breakup can leave you feeling isolated and alone. Reconnecting with your support system fosters a sense of belonging and reminds you that you're not alone in navigating this difficult journey. Knowing others care about you and are there for you can significantly reduce feelings of loneliness and isolation, creating a safety net and a space for emotional expression.

Example: After Olivia's breakup, she initially retreated into isolation, avoiding social contact. However, she soon recognized the negative impact of loneliness on her emotional well-being. She reached out to a close friend who invited her for a weekend getaway. Spending time with her friend, reminiscing about happy memories and sharing her current challenges, helped Olivia feel less alone and more connected.

- **Validation and Encouragement:** Sharing your experiences with a supportive friend, family member, or therapist allows them to offer validation for your emotions and experiences. Hearing someone say, "Your feelings are valid," can be incredibly comforting and empowering. Additionally, receiving words of encouragement and reminders of your strength can boost your confidence and motivation to move forward.

Example: David, feeling defeated after the breakup, confided in his supportive brother. His brother listened patiently and offered validation for David's emotions. He also reminded David of his past accomplishments and resilience, highlighting his ability to overcome challenges. This conversation helped David feel validated and empowered to navigate the difficulties ahead.

- **Stress Reduction and Improved Well-being:** Social interaction stimulates the release of oxytocin, a neurotransmitter associated with feelings of happiness, bonding, and trust. Spending time with loved ones can offer a welcome distraction from negative emotions, allowing for moments of joy and relaxation. Sharing laughter, engaging in lighthearted activities, or simply enjoying each other's company can significantly reduce stress and promote overall emotional well-being.

Example: Sarah, overwhelmed with sadness, decided to join a weekly game night with her friends. Playing board games, laughing with friends, and enjoying their company provided a much-needed escape from her emotional turmoil. The social interaction and the positive atmosphere helped Sarah feel lighter and temporarily alleviate her stress.

Reconnecting with Your Diverse Support System

Your support system doesn't have to be one-dimensional. It can encompass a diverse range of individuals who enrich your life and offer different kinds of support. Here are ways to reconnect and build a strong support system:

- **Friends:** Reach out to close friends who offer a non-judgmental space to express your emotions. Share your experiences, ask for support, and engage in activities you enjoy together. Friends can provide companionship, understanding, and a sense of normalcy during difficult times.
- **Family:** Family members can offer a sense of belonging and unconditional love. If you have a good relationship with your family, consider confiding in them and seeking their support. Family gatherings can also provide a sense of connection and a break from the emotional intensity of the breakup.

Example: After his breakup, David reached out to his sister, someone he always confided in. Talking openly about his emotions and receiving her understanding and support helped David feel better connected and less alone. Additionally, he started having weekly dinners with his parents, creating a sense of normalcy and reminding him of the enduring love of his family.

- **Support Groups:** Connecting with individuals who have experienced similar situations can be incredibly valuable. Support groups offer a safe space to share your experiences, learn from others, and feel a sense of belonging. You'll gain the comfort of knowing you're not alone and receive valuable insights from individuals who have navigated similar challenges.

Example: Olivia, struggling to move on from her breakup, decided to join a local support group for individuals going through breakups. Sharing her experiences and listening to others' stories helped Olivia feel a sense of connection and belonging. It also provided her with a platform to learn healthy coping mechanisms from others further along in their healing journey.

- **Professional Help:** A therapist or counselor can offer invaluable support and guidance on your journey towards healing. Therapy provides a safe space to explore your emotions, develop healthy coping mechanisms, and learn strategies for moving forward in a healthy way. A therapist can also help you identify any underlying patterns or issues that may have contributed to the relationship's end, empowering you to make healthier choices in future relationships.

Example: Sarah, struggling with overwhelming emotions and difficulty managing daily life after her breakup, decided to seek professional help. Through therapy, Sarah learned healthy coping mechanisms for managing her emotions, such as mindfulness meditation and journaling. She also explored underlying issues that might have contributed to the relationship's end, allowing her to gain valuable insights for future relationships.

Building a Strong and Sustainable Support System:

Building a strong support system takes time, effort, and intentionality. Here are some tips for fostering and maintaining a supportive network:

- **Be Open and Honest:** Building genuine connections requires vulnerability and honesty. Share your experiences and feelings authentically with those you trust.
- **Respect Boundaries:** Everyone has their own capacity for emotional support. Be mindful of your loved ones' limitations and respect their boundaries. Don't overload them with your emotional baggage.
- **Reciprocity is Key:** A healthy support system is a two-way street. Offer support and care to others in your network as well.

- **Expand Your Network:** While reconnecting with existing relationships is crucial, don't be afraid to expand your social circle. Join clubs, volunteer, or take classes to meet new people who share similar interests.
- **Practice Self-Care:** Prioritize your own well-being. Engage in activities that bring you joy and nourish your mind, body, and spirit. Taking care of yourself empowers you to better care for and connect with others.

Remember:

- **Healing is not linear:** There will be good days and bad days. Be patient with yourself, allow yourself to feel your emotions, and don't be discouraged by setbacks.
- **Not everyone will be supportive:** Some individuals may not be equipped or willing to offer the level of support you need. Let go of expectations and focus on nurturing genuine connections with those who truly understand and support you.
- **You are not alone:** Remember that countless individuals have navigated the challenges of a breakup and emerged stronger. Embrace the support offered by your network, and trust that with time and effort, you will heal and move forward towards a brighter future.

By reconnecting with your support system and building a diverse network of individuals who offer various kinds of support, you create a powerful force on your healing journey. The love, understanding, and encouragement from loved ones, along with professional guidance if needed, can provide a safe harbor during emotional storms and propel you towards a future filled with connection, well-being, and personal growth.

Remember, the strength to heal lies within you and is amplified by the support of those who care!

Chapter 8: Charting New Courses - Exploring New Possibilities

The aftermath of a breakup can feel like the rug has been pulled out from under you, leaving you adrift in a sea of uncertainty. Everything you thought you knew about your future might be in question. However, this period of transition also presents a unique opportunity for self-discovery and growth.

In Chapter 8, we'll encourage you to embrace the power of exploration – a chance to "chart new courses" by delving into new interests, hobbies, or even career paths. This journey of exploration can reignite your passions, foster personal development, and open doors to unexpected possibilities.

A Turning Point: Why Exploration Matters After a Breakup

A breakup can be a pivotal moment in your life. It can disrupt your sense of self, your routines, and your social circle. While the initial period might be filled with grief and sadness, it also presents a chance to hit the reset button and redefine who you are outside of the relationship. Here's why exploration matters in the healing process:

- **Rediscovering Your Passions:** Often, relationships involve compromise and adjustments. You might have neglected hobbies or interests due to time constraints or to prioritize your partner's preferences. Exploring new possibilities allows you to reconnect with yourself, rediscover neglected passions, and uncover hidden talents. This process can be incredibly rewarding and remind you of the things that bring you joy outside of a relationship.

Example: Daniel, who had always put his career goals on hold to support his ex-partner's artistic aspirations, decided to revisit his passion for writing after the breakup. He enrolled in a creative writing course, reconnected with his creative side, and discovered a renewed sense of purpose and fulfillment through writing.

- **Boosting Confidence and Self-Esteem:** Learning new skills or mastering a new hobby can be a significant confidence booster. The sense of accomplishment that comes from achieving goals in new areas fuels self-belief and empowers you to explore other possibilities. The challenges and triumphs you experience during exploration contribute to a deeper understanding of your strengths and capabilities.

Example: Sarah, who always felt hesitant to try public speaking because of her ex-partner's criticism, decided to join a Toastmasters club after the breakup. By overcoming her fear and developing her presentation skills, Sarah gained confidence that spilled over into other areas of her life. She discovered a newfound ability to advocate for herself and express her ideas with clarity and conviction.

- **Expanding Your Social Circle:** Exploring new interests often involves joining clubs, taking classes, or volunteering for causes you care about. These activities provide opportunities to meet like-minded individuals and build new friendships based on shared passions. Expanding your social circle can combat feelings of loneliness and isolation, introduce you to new perspectives, and create a support system based on shared interests.

Example: Olivia, wanting to explore her passion for hiking after the breakup, joined a local hiking group. Through these outings, she met new people who shared her love for nature and formed meaningful friendships. These connections not only enriched her social life but also offered a sense of camaraderie and shared experiences.

Embarking on Your Exploration Journey: A Sea of Exciting Possibilities

The possibilities for exploration are vast and limited only by your imagination. Here are some ideas to spark your curiosity and ignite your journey of self-discovery:

- **Travel:** Immersing yourself in new cultures, exploring historical sites, or simply escaping the familiar can broaden your perspective and inspire you. Whether it's a weekend getaway to a nearby city, a backpacking trip across continents, or a solo adventure to a new country, travel provides opportunities for personal growth and unforgettable experiences. It can challenge you to step outside your comfort zone, navigate unfamiliar situations, and develop new skills like basic communication in another language.

Example: David, who had always dreamed of experiencing the vibrant culture of Southeast Asia, decided to book a solo backpacking trip after the breakup. Traveling through Thailand, Vietnam, and Cambodia, he immersed himself in the local customs, tried exotic cuisines, and explored ancient temples. This solo adventure not only fulfilled a lifelong dream but also fostered independence, adaptability, and a deeper appreciation for different cultures.

- **Learning New Skills:** Have you always wanted to learn a new language, play an instrument, master a particular software program, or even delve into coding? Now is the perfect time to invest in yourself and acquire new skills that can benefit your personal and professional life. Numerous online courses, workshops, and classes cater to almost any interest, from learning basic photography to mastering advanced woodworking techniques. This investment in your skillset can not only bring personal satisfaction but also open doors to new career opportunities in the future.

Example: After the breakup, Sarah decided to enroll in an online course on graphic design, a field that had always intrigued her. She dedicated time each week to learning the fundamentals of design software, color theory, and layout principles. As her skills developed, she found herself enjoying the creative process and the sense of accomplishment that came with completing projects. This newfound passion not only provided an outlet for her creativity but also opened doors to freelance design opportunities in the future.

- **Revisit Old Passions:** Perhaps you neglected a hobby due to time constraints or relationship dynamics during your previous relationship. Dust off that old guitar, enroll in a dance class you always wanted to try, or revisit any creative pursuit that sparked joy in the past. Reconnecting with your old passions can reignite excitement, offer comfort during challenging times, and remind you of the things that bring you fulfillment outside of a romantic relationship.

Example: Daniel, who used to enjoy playing the piano in his youth, rediscovered his passion for music after the breakup. He started practicing again, enrolled in piano lessons to refresh his skills, and even joined a local community choir. Reconnecting with his musical side brought him immense joy, provided a healthy outlet for stress, and allowed him to connect with other music enthusiasts in the community.

- **Volunteer Your Time:** Giving back to the community can be incredibly fulfilling and provide a sense of purpose, especially during a time when you might be questioning your own direction. Volunteer opportunities are available for almost any cause you care about, allowing you to connect with others while making a positive impact on the world. Volunteering can expose you to new experiences, develop valuable skills, and foster a sense of belonging to a larger community.

Example: Olivia, wanting to contribute to a cause she cared about, decided to volunteer at a local animal shelter after the breakup. Walking dogs, playing with cats, and assisting with other shelter duties provided her with a sense of purpose and helped her connect with other animal lovers. Volunteering not only offered comfort and companionship during a difficult time but also allowed her to make a positive difference in the lives of animals in need.

- **Career Exploration:** A breakup can prompt you to re-evaluate your career path and consider if your current job aligns with your values and long-term aspirations. This period of self-discovery is an ideal time to explore new career options. Consider taking online courses, attending career workshops, or connecting with professionals in fields that pique your interest. This exploration might lead to a career change or simply a renewed enthusiasm for your current path, knowing that it aligns with your evolving goals and aspirations.

Example: Sarah, who had been working in marketing for several years, realized after the breakup that she longed for a more creative career outlet. She started researching different creative fields, took online courses in web design and content creation, and even connected with freelance content creators to gain insights into the industry. This exploration process helped her clarify her career goals and set her on a path towards a more fulfilling professional future.

Remember:

- **Don't be afraid to step outside your comfort zone:** Personal growth often happens beyond your comfort zone. Embrace the challenges and uncertainties that come with exploring new things. Stepping outside your comfort zone can lead to unexpected discoveries, hidden talents, and a deeper understanding of yourself.

- **Start small and celebrate your progress:** Trying too much too soon can lead to overwhelm. Begin with small, manageable goals, such as taking an introductory class or joining a local meetup group related to your interests. Celebrate your progress along the way, no matter how small, as each step forward is a victory in your exploration journey.

- **Focus on the journey, not the destination:** The process of exploration is just as important as the outcome. Enjoy the learning experience, the new skills you acquire, the people you meet, and the unexpected detours along the way. Embrace the journey of self-discovery with an open mind and a curious spirit.

Conclusion:

The period following a breakup, while challenging, can be a catalyst for self-discovery and growth. By "charting new courses" and exploring new possibilities, you open yourself to a world of exciting experiences, personal development, and a renewed sense of purpose. Embrace the journey, invest in yourself, and trust that new beginnings and unexpected joys await you on this exciting path of exploration.

Remember, you are capable of achieving incredible things, and your future holds endless possibilities. As you embark on this exploration journey, remember that growth and transformation take time. Be patient with yourself, celebrate your victories, and embrace the exciting possibilities that lie ahead.

Chapter 9: Embracing the Open Seas - Finding Gratitude and Optimism

The aftermath of a breakup can feel like being caught in a sudden storm at sea. The familiar landscape is obscured by choppy waves, and uncertainty looms large on the horizon. However, amidst the turbulence lies the strength and resilience to navigate these challenging waters.

In Chapter 9, we'll guide you towards "embracing the open seas" by cultivating gratitude for past experiences and the lessons learned. We'll also encourage you to adopt an optimistic outlook as you set sail towards a brighter future.

The Power of Gratitude: Finding Strength in Thankfulness

Gratitude is often associated with expressing thanks for positive experiences. But its power extends far beyond that. Cultivating gratitude during challenging times can be a transformative force, offering a powerful anchor in the emotional storm of a breakup. Here's why incorporating gratitude into your healing journey is vital:

- **Shifting the Perspective Compass:** When you focus on what you're grateful for, even during difficult times, it shifts your perspective from negativity to appreciation. This allows you to acknowledge the positive aspects of your life, fostering a sense of optimism and hope. Just as a sailor uses a compass to navigate, cultivating gratitude helps you find direction and focus on the positive aspects that guide you forward.

Example: Sarah, feeling overwhelmed and consumed by negativity after the breakup, decided to create a daily "gratitude log." Each morning, she wrote down three things she was grateful for, including small things like a warm cup of coffee, a beautiful sunrise, or a supportive friend who listened without judgment. This practice of acknowledging the good in her life, however small, helped her shift her focus from the pain of the breakup to the positive aspects that offered her comfort and a sense of stability.

- **Embracing Growth and Learning as Treasures from the Journey:** Relationships, even those that end, offer valuable lessons and opportunities for growth. Cultivating gratitude allows you to appreciate the personal development and knowledge gained from the experience. Focusing on the lessons learned empowers you to navigate future relationships with greater clarity and wisdom. Just like finding hidden treasures on a journey, the lessons learned from your past relationship can equip you for a brighter future.

Example: David, reflecting on his past relationship, realized that he had neglected his own needs in an attempt to prioritize his ex-partner's happiness. While acknowledging the pain of the breakup, he also expressed gratitude for the experience, as it highlighted the importance of self-care and assertive communication in future relationships. This newfound awareness became a valuable treasure he carried forward, empowering him to build healthier connections in the future.

- **Strengthening Your Inner Resilience: Gratitude as Your Life Raft:** Gratitude fosters a sense of resilience, the ability to bounce back from challenges. By acknowledging the good in your life, you cultivate inner strength and optimism, enabling you to navigate difficult emotions and move forward with a positive attitude. Gratitude acts as a life raft in the stormy seas, providing stability and buoyancy amidst emotional turbulence.

Example: Olivia, reflecting on the positive aspects of her past relationship, felt a surge of gratitude for the shared experiences and the personal growth she had experienced. This gratitude strengthened her resilience and instilled a sense of optimism as she looked towards the future. She knew, deep down, that she had the strength to overcome challenges and experience new love, carrying the lessons learned from her past relationship as a guiding light.

Developing Your Gratitude Practice: Tools for Navigation

Cultivating gratitude is a practice that can be incorporated into your daily life, equipping you with valuable tools for navigating the seas of healing. Here are some ways to embark on your gratitude journey:

- **Gratitude Journaling: Charting Your Course:** Set aside a few minutes each day to write down three things you're grateful for, big or small. This could be a beautiful sunrise, a supportive friend who listened without judgment, a delicious meal, or even the strength and resilience you possess. Do this first thing in the morning to set a positive tone for the day, or before bed to reflect on the day's blessings.

- **Gratitude Meditation: Finding Calm in the Storm:** Meditation practices incorporating gratitude can be incredibly calming and uplifting. Find a quiet space, focus on your breath, and visualize the things you're grateful for. Send feelings of appreciation towards yourself, loved ones, or even aspects of your life you appreciate. This practice creates a calm oasis amidst the emotional storm, fostering peace and a sense of well-being.

- **Sharing Gratitude: Sending Appreciation Signals:** Verbally expressing your gratitude to friends, family, or even yourself can be incredibly powerful. Take a moment to thank a friend for their support, write a gratitude note to a past mentor, or simply tell yourself what you appreciate about yourself. Sharing your gratitude strengthens your connections with others and reinforces your own sense of positivity.

Embracing Optimism: Setting Sail for a Brighter Future

Optimism is the belief that things will turn out well, even when faced with challenges. It's the wind in your sails, propelling you forward with the confidence and motivation to navigate towards a brighter future. After a breakup, embracing optimism can be a powerful tool for healing and setting sail towards a fulfilling life.

Fueling Hope and Motivation: Setting the Course for a Brighter Horizon

Optimism fosters hope for a brighter future, even when the present feels bleak. It provides the motivation to move forward, set new goals, and create a future filled with positive possibilities. Just as a sailor sets a course based on the stars, optimism guides you towards a desired destination, offering the motivation to overcome obstacles and navigate challenges along the way.

Example: David, despite feeling emotional pain after the breakup, embraced optimism by focusing on the future. He set new personal and professional goals, reconnected with old friends, and started exploring new hobbies. This optimistic outlook fueled his motivation to create a fulfilling life for himself, propelling him forward with a sense of purpose and direction.

- **Enhancing Positive Experiences:** An optimistic mindset allows you to approach new opportunities with a positive perspective. This openness can enhance your experiences, allowing you to connect with new people, discover new interests, and create new and lasting positive memories. Just as experiencing favorable weather conditions on a voyage can enhance the journey, optimism allows you to savor the positive aspects of life and create memories filled with joy and fulfillment.

Example: Sarah, feeling optimistic after focusing on gratitude, joined a local dance class. Her positive attitude allowed her to embrace the learning process, connect with other classmates who shared her passion for dance, and experience the joy of movement. This newfound joy enriched her life in unexpected ways, creating positive experiences that would shape her future.

- **Building Resilience: Weathering the Storms with Optimism as Your Anchor** Optimism, like gratitude, strengthens your resilience in the face of challenges. A positive mindset allows you to view setbacks as temporary obstacles rather than insurmountable roadblocks. This helps you persevere through difficult times and continue to strive towards your goals. Just as a strong anchor keeps a ship steady during a storm, optimism helps you weather the storms of life with perseverance and a sense of hope.

Example: Olivia, facing challenges during her job search after the breakup, maintained an optimistic outlook. She focused on her skills and qualifications, actively applied for jobs, and used each interview as a learning experience. This optimism helped her bounce back from rejections and maintain the motivation to continue her search until she landed a fulfilling job, demonstrating the power of optimism in navigating life's challenges with resilience and determination.

Cultivating Optimism in Daily Life: Tools for Strengthening Your Sail

Here are some ways to cultivate optimism in your daily life, strengthening your sail for navigating the seas of life:

- **Challenge Negative Thoughts: Reframing Your Perspective:** When negative thoughts arise, challenge their validity and reframe them into more positive perspectives. Focus on the possibilities and potential solutions instead of dwelling on worst-case scenarios. Just as a sailor adjusts the sails based on the changing winds, learn to adjust your perspective and reframe negative thoughts into positive ones.

- **Focus on the Positive: Appreciating the Sunshine on Your Journey:** Make a conscious effort to focus on the positive aspects of your life, however small they may seem. Celebrate your victories, no matter how big or small, and acknowledge the good things you have going for you. This focus on the positive aspects of your life serves as sunshine on your journey, propelling you forward with a sense of optimism and joy.

- **Surround Yourself with Positive People: Choosing Your Crew Wisely:** Spend time with people who uplift and inspire you. Their positive energy can be contagious and help you maintain a positive outlook on life. Just as a supportive crew is essential for a successful voyage, surrounding yourself with positive people creates a supportive environment that fosters optimism and growth.

Conclusion: Embracing the Journey with Gratitude and Optimism

Moving forward from a breakup requires both emotional healing and a shift in perspective. By cultivating gratitude for the past and embracing optimism for the future, you equip yourself with powerful tools for navigating this challenging chapter. Remember, gratitude allows you to find strength and appreciate the lessons learned, while optimism fuels hope and motivates you to create a brighter future.

Embrace the journey, cultivate these positive mindsets, and set sail towards a future filled with new possibilities and endless opportunities for growth and happiness. Just as a skilled sailor navigates the seas using their compass and the wind in their sails, you too can navigate the journey of healing and growth with gratitude and optimism as your guiding lights.

Remember, even the stormiest seas can lead you to beautiful and uncharted destinations.

Chapter 10: Finding Your True North - Building Healthy Relationships

The aftermath of a breakup can feel like a disorienting journey through unfamiliar territory. The map you once relied on, filled with expectations and assumptions about relationships, might seem outdated or even misleading. However, amidst this uncertainty lies an opportunity for self-discovery.

In Chapter 10, we'll guide you towards finding your "true north" – a set of core values and expectations that will guide you towards building healthy and fulfilling relationships in the future. Here, we'll delve deeper into understanding healthy relationship expectations and setting healthy boundaries.

Charting Your Course: Defining Healthy Relationship Expectations

Healthy relationship expectations are more than just a wish list. They are the fundamental qualities and values you seek in a partner. Defining these expectations allows you to approach future relationships with clarity and avoid compromising your well-being. Here's a roadmap to help you identify your healthy relationship expectations:

- **Embark on a Voyage of Self-Discovery:** Take time for introspection. Journal about your past relationships, both positive and negative. Identify what worked and what didn't. List the qualities you truly value in a partner. What are your dealbreakers? What are the non-negotiables that you will not compromise on in a relationship? This journey of self-reflection helps you understand your needs, desires, and values, which act as the guiding stars for your relationship compass.

Example: Sarah, after reflecting on her past relationship, realized that she had often prioritized her partner's needs over her own. Through introspection, she discovered that she valued honesty, open communication, and shared interests in a partner. However, she also identified financial responsibility, emotional maturity, and mutual respect as non-negotiables. Equipped with this newfound clarity, she embarked on her journey towards building healthy relationships.

- **Open Communication: Setting Sail with Honesty:** Don't be afraid to openly communicate your expectations to potential partners. As you get to know someone, have honest conversations about your values, communication styles, goals for the relationship, and even your financial outlook. Clear communication sets the tone for a healthy and respectful partnership from the very beginning. It allows you to assess compatibility and identify potential areas of concern before investing deeply in the relationship.

Example: David, after experiencing a relationship where his partner had different life goals, decided to prioritize open communication about his own aspirations. When dating, he actively sought partners who shared his interest in travel and personal growth. He also openly communicated his desire for a future partnership built on mutual support and shared life goals. This honest communication allowed him to connect with potential partners who were compatible with his long-term vision.

Healthy Relationship Expectations: Anchoring Your Values

Here are some key aspects to consider when defining your healthy relationship expectations:

- **Shared Values:** Do you share core values such as honesty, respect, and kindness? Do you have similar outlooks on life, family, and finances? Shared values create a foundation of trust and understanding, fostering a sense of security and connection within the relationship.

- **Communication Styles:** Do you communicate openly and honestly? Do you actively listen to each other and respect each other's perspectives? Healthy communication styles allow for constructive conflict resolution and foster a safe space for emotional connection.

- **Emotional Compatibility:** Do you feel emotionally supported and understood by your partner? Do you share similar levels of emotional intelligence and maturity? Emotional compatibility allows for deeper intimacy and creates a supportive environment for individual growth.

- **Mutual Respect:** Is your partner respectful of your boundaries, needs, and decisions? Do you feel valued and appreciated for who you are? Mutual respect is the cornerstone of any healthy relationship, fostering trust and creating a safe space for both partners to thrive.

- **Shared Life Goals:** Do you have compatible long-term goals? Do you envision a future together that aligns with your individual aspirations? Shared life goals provide a sense of direction and purpose for the relationship, fostering a sense of partnership and commitment.

Remember: Your expectations are not static. As you evolve and grow as a person, your expectations might also change. It's important to be open to reevaluating your expectations throughout your life and to communicate these changes with your partner.

Building Healthy Boundaries: Safeguarding Your Emotional Well-Being

Boundaries are essential in any relationship. They create a safe space for individual growth and mutual respect. Healthy boundaries define acceptable behavior and protect your physical and emotional well-being. Here's how to establish healthy boundaries:

- **Charting Your Inner Landscape:** Identify your personal needs and limitations. What behaviors make you feel uncomfortable or disrespected? What level of communication and emotional support do you need? How much alone time do you require to feel healthy and balanced? Understanding your needs allows you to set boundaries that protect your well-being and create a foundation for a healthy and fulfilling relationship.

- **Communicating Your Boundaries with Clarity:** Once you understand your needs, communicate your boundaries assertively and respectfully. Be clear, concise, and avoid using accusatory language. Focus on "I" statements and express your needs calmly and directly. For example, instead of saying, "You're always calling me late," you could say, "I feel disrespected when our plans change last minute. It would be helpful if you could call me earlier if something comes up."

Example: Olivia, after experiencing emotional manipulation in a past relationship, set a clear boundary regarding respecting her personal space and need for alone time. She communicated this need to her partners, stating that she valued open communication but also needed respect for her need for independent time. She emphasized that this wasn't a reflection on the relationship but a way for her to maintain her mental and emotional well-being. This clear communication helped her partners understand her needs and fostered a more respectful dynamic within the relationship.

Recognizing Red Flags: Navigating Unhealthy Relationship Dynamics

It's crucial to be aware of red flags – behaviors or patterns that indicate an unhealthy relationship dynamic. These red flags can serve as warning signs, prompting you to re-evaluate the relationship and prioritize your well-being. Here are some common red flags to watch out for:

- **Disrespect:** This can manifest in various forms, including name-calling, belittling, put-downs, sarcasm, or any behavior that undermines your self-esteem and emotional well-being.
- **Manipulation:** This involves controlling your behavior, using guilt or fear to get what they want, isolating you from your support system, or gaslighting you into questioning your reality.
- **Jealousy and Possessiveness:** Unhealthy levels of jealousy or possessiveness can be controlling and suffocating. This behavior often stems from insecurity and can limit your freedom and autonomy within the relationship.
- **Lack of Communication:** Inability to communicate openly and honestly, or dismissing your feelings and concerns, can hinder a healthy relationship. Open communication is essential for building trust, resolving conflicts constructively, and fostering emotional intimacy.
- **Abuse:** Physical, emotional, verbal, or sexual abuse is never acceptable in any relationship. If you are experiencing any form of abuse, seek help from a trusted friend, family member, or professional immediately.

Remember: You deserve to be treated with respect, honesty, and kindness. If you encounter any red flags, prioritize your well-being and do not hesitate to walk away from the relationship.

Building Your Relationship Compass: Setting Sail for a Fulfilling Journey

By understanding your healthy relationship expectations and setting clear boundaries, you equip yourself with a compass and map to navigate the journey towards building fulfilling relationships. Remember, a healthy relationship:

- *Prioritizes mutual respect and understanding.*
- *Provides a safe space for individual growth and emotional vulnerability.*
- *Fosters open and honest communication.*
- *Supports your individual goals and aspirations.*
- *Enhances your overall well-being and happiness.*

Remember:

- **Invest in Self-Care:** Prioritize your personal growth and well-being. This strengthens you emotionally and empowers you to make healthy choices in your relationships. Engage in activities that bring you joy, nurture your physical and mental health, and surround yourself with supportive people.
- **Be Patient:** Building healthy relationships takes time and effort. Don't rush into commitments and trust your intuition when evaluating potential partners. Allow yourself to get to know someone gradually and prioritize building a foundation of trust and shared values.
- **Communicate Openly and Honestly:** Honest and respectful communication is the foundation of any healthy relationship. Express your needs and desires clearly, listen actively to your partner, and be open to compromise and collaboration.

Moving forward after a breakup can be challenging, but it's also an opportunity for immense personal growth.

By defining your "true north" through healthy expectations and boundaries, you pave the way for building healthy, fulfilling, and lasting relationships in the future.

Remember, you are worthy of love, respect, and a partner who complements your journey towards a happy and fulfilling life. Embrace the journey, trust your intuition, and set sail towards building relationships that enrich your life and support your growth.

Conclusion

The journey through heartbreak can feel like navigating uncharted territory, the familiar landscape obscured by emotional storms. But amidst the pain and uncertainty, lies immense opportunity for growth and personal transformation. As you close this chapter, remember the ten guiding principles you've explored:

1. **Acknowledge Your Emotions:** Validate your feelings and allow yourself to grieve the loss.
2. **Seek Support:** Surround yourself with loved ones who can offer comfort and understanding.
3. **Practice Self-Care:** Prioritize your physical and mental well-being through healthy habits and activities that nourish your soul.
4. **Embrace Forgiveness:** Forgive yourself and your ex-partner, not to condone their actions, but to release yourself from the burden of resentment.
5. **Learn from the Experience:** Reflect on the lessons learned and use them to become a stronger, wiser individual.
6. **Reconnect with Yourself:** Rediscover your passions, interests, and desires, and nurture the unique qualities that make you special.
7. **Celebrate Your Independence:** Embrace your newfound freedom and enjoy the opportunities to explore new experiences and forge new paths.
8. **Cultivate Gratitude:** Appreciate the positive aspects of your life, both big and small, fostering a sense of optimism and hope.
9. **Embrace Optimism:** Believe in your ability to heal, grow, and experience love again.

10. **Find Your True North:** Define your healthy relationship expectations and set clear boundaries to guide you towards fulfilling connections.

Remember, you are stronger and more resilient than you might feel right now. The pain of the present will not last forever. With time, patience, and self-compassion, you will heal and emerge from this experience with newfound strength and wisdom.

Embrace the journey of self-discovery, and trust your unwavering inner compass to guide you towards a brighter future filled with love, happiness, and fulfilling connections. Remember, even the stormiest seas can lead you to beautiful and uncharted destinations.

The End.

Don't miss out!

Visit the website below and you can sign up to receive emails whenever Pasindu A publishes a new book. There's no charge and no obligation.

https://books2read.com/r/B-A-BEABB-XRYYC

BOOKS 2 READ

Connecting independent readers to independent writers.

Did you love *Love's Broken Compass: Reclaiming Your Direction After a Heartbreak*? Then you should read *Find the Man of Your Dreams: 10 Traits of High-Value Men*[1] by Pasindu A!

[2]

Find the Man of Your Dreams: 10 Traits of High-Value Men

Are you tired of dating the wrong guys? Are you looking for a man who is intelligent, kind, supportive, and ambitious? If so, then this book is for you!

In this book, you will learn about the 10 traits of high-value men in relationships. These traits are:

Integrity and moral courageEmotional intelligenceConfidence and self-assurednessContinuous personal growthEmpathy and compassionIndependence and self-relianceResilience and adaptabilityRespectful and supportive natureHumility and

---

1. https://books2read.com/u/bOeM1N

2. https://books2read.com/u/bOeM1N

gratitudeLeadership and empowerment

You will learn how to spot these traits in a man, and how to attract and keep a high-value man in your life.

This book is essential reading for any woman who is serious about finding and keeping the man of her dreams. It is also a valuable resource for men who want to become the best partners they can be.

Here are just a few of the benefits of reading this book:

You will learn how to avoid dating the wrong guys and focus on dating high-value men.You will learn how to spot the signs of a high-value man.You will learn how to attract and keep a high-value man in your life.You will learn how to build a strong and healthy relationship with a high-value man.You will learn how to create a life that is full of love, happiness, and fulfillment.

If you are ready to find the man of your dreams, then order your copy of this book today!

If you are a man who wants to become more attractive to women and become the best version of yourself,

This book will teach you the 10 traits of high-value men and how to develop them. It will also teach you how to become more attractive to women and how to build strong and healthy relationships.

If you are ready to become the best version of yourself, then order your copy of this book today!

Read more at https://healthfactsbydoctorpasindu.com/.

Also by Pasindu A

Find the Man of Your Dreams: 10 Traits of High-Value Men
Miles Apart Hearts Together: 10 Ways to Thrive in a Long Distance Relationship
Financial Planning for the Modern Couple: 10 Ways to Manage Your Finances in Today's Economy
The Disaster Preparedness Survival Guide: 10 Tips on How to Plan and Prepare for Any Emergency
The Secret to a Great Sex Life
The Science of Attraction
Love's Broken Compass: Reclaiming Your Direction After a Heartbreak

Watch for more at https://healthfactsbydoctorpasindu.com/.

About the Author

Pasindu A is a passionate writer, a doctor, and a relationship expert. Heis the author of several ebooks on self-improvement and relationships,including the popular ebook "Find the Man of Your Dreams: 10 Traitsof High-Value Men."Pasindu A is a gifted writer with a unique ability to connect with hisreaders and help them achieve their goals.

Follow him on Facebook and Instagram - "healthfactsbydoctorpasindu"

Read more at https://www.facebook.com/healthfactsbydoctorpasindu?mibextid=ibOpuV.

9 798224 926992